# Isadora
# Duncan

Isadora Duncan. Photo by Arnold Genthe. New York, 1916.

# Isadora Duncan

EDITED BY PAUL MAGRIEL

HENRY HOLT AND COMPANY • NEW YORK

# PREFACE

THE YEAR 1947 marks the twentieth anniversary of the death of a distinguished American dancer, Isadora Duncan. An embodiment of the American spirit, fearless, honest and direct, with a burning love of freedom, she passionately believed in dancing as the great art. Indeed her first awareness of herself was as a dancer—a dancer who wanted to move freely and embrace the whole of humanity. She was in a sense our first American dancer since those in this country who preceded her—Mary Ann Lee, Augusta Maywood, George Washington Smith and others—were concerned primarily with the formal European tradition of theatrical dancing. It was Isadora who first brought to Europe and then to her own country, a new attitude—her own vision of America Dancing.

Isadora's particular genius as a person as well as an artist has probably evoked more contemporary interest than any other theatrical personality of her time. The legend that she has left is still subject to special scrutiny and the particular school that followed her (although she was personally against the notion of schools and traditions) based on her "technique" is today probably not at all a reflection of her principles and style, since these were qualities inherent in Isadora, the person and artist, and hence were nontransferable. However, in the vast body of contemporary modern dance her notions on dancing are widely manifested and it is apparent that her indirect influence on Fokine and subsequently the Russian Ballet have made possible certain innovations which persist today.

In this series of essays and commentaries on Isadora there is further evidence of her unique personality and greatness. The notes on her early concerts in New York are as fresh and vital after thirty years as if they had been written yesterday, while the comments on Isadora and basic dance contribute more substantially to our understanding of her than anything which has appeared since her autobiography. The interest in her as a subject for artists is indicated in the range of paintings, drawings, and sketches which are reproduced in this book. These together with the various photographs illuminate in some measure the quality of Isadora the dancer and of her boundless personality.

# ACKNOWLEDGMENTS

THE MATERIAL in this book is made up largely from issues of the periodical, *Dance Index*, and I am grateful to Mr. John Martin, Mr. Carl Van Vechten, and Mr. Allan Ross Macdougall who have graciously given me their permission for the use of this unique material. I am also indebted to *The New York Times* for permission to reprint Mr. Van Vechten's pieces on Isadora which appeared in *The New York Times* on the dates noted in the article. I acknowledge with thanks the permission of Alfred A. Knopf to reprint *The New Isadora*, which first appeared in Carl Van Vechten's book *The Merry-Go-Round*, 1918. Captain Edward Steichen has permitted me to publish his excellent photograph of Isadora at the Parthenon, and Mr. George Chaffee has been kind enough to loan me the study of Isadora by Gordon Craig. Mr. George Amberg of the Department of Theatre Arts, the Museum of Modern Art, has made available to me the excellent material in his department and Mr. Edwin Denby located two rare photographs of Isadora taken in Munich. It is through their courtesies that this book is being published and to them I extend my warmest thanks.

# CONTENTS

# Isadora Duncan

# Isadora Duncan and Basic Dance

## AN OUTLINE FOR DANCERS

### BY JOHN MARTIN

IT IS a curious thing that in all the reams that have been written about Isadora Duncan there is so little with any specific bearing upon her art. There are tributes aplenty, eulogies and poems, word-pictures of the personal states she inspired in her spectators, and romantics of all kinds frequently bordering on the fulsome, but virtually nothing is to be found that examines objectively what she did and sets it forth in orderly terms with reference to its permanent values and formulable principles. To all intents she might have been a transient phenomenon floating across time in her scarves to no more purpose than a meteor. Yet actually she is greater now than she was while her comparatively short and stormy career was going on, and will become greater still as the inertia of mass thinking continues to dissolve with the passing of time and the import of her accomplishment becomes clearer.

She herself saw but was, of course, never reconciled to the unavoidability of this time lapse. Of her countrymen she asked rhetorically from overseas when they would quit neglecting her, see the purpose of her work and make it possible for her to carry on; and she answered her own question with the prophecy that fifty years after her death they would build a monument to her. Less than fifteen of these years have yet gone by but the prophecy is already beginning to be fulfilled. The monument that is building,

I

however, is not the conventional tribute in stone which she foresaw, but a body of living dance freely acknowledging her as its source. It is still struggling as she struggled against indifference, to some extent, but what is more of a handicap, it is still working largely through intuition as she was forced to work, in spite of the fact that her very efforts have made this no longer a necessity.

Isadora has left scattered through her brief writings a fully rounded theory of the dance which is generally not suspected, and it is time to add to the already crowded bookshelf devoted to her one volume which undertakes to look beyond personality and to order and elucidate this material. Such a task adequately performed would result in probably the greatest textbook of the dance ever written. It is not to be accomplished, however, by him who writes as he runs. It demands insight into an altogether intuitive mind pitting itself against respected inertias and entrenched bigotries; it further demands courage to read between the lines in order to see the things that Isadora herself did not know she saw, and to penetrate the surface limitations of a period as well as of an individual who, though she belongs among the great ones of the earth, had her prejudices and predilections, conscious and unconscious. It is a job for an intensely practical mind, able not only to extract the universal theory from a highly personal art, but, once that is done, to reparticularize it in terms of contemporary practice.

This would entail discoveries and adaptations that would surprise and shock Isadora herself, if she could learn of them, for great concepts frequently grow beyond the grasp of those who have earliest enunciated them. Take, for example, the way we talk today of democracy not only as a political and social philosophy, but also as an economic one, and compare it with the ideas of so notable a pioneering democrat as Thomas Jefferson, who was not even in favor of universal male suffrage. Yet it is the same concept, acted upon by the changing demands of the times and by its own growth from within. Our textbook compiler must be able to establish as definite a nucleus of Isadora's fundamental concept and keep it clear through its various changes of aspect in her own and others' application of it. Especially must he be wary of the roseate mist that surrounded it in the days of its birth. Isadora "freed" the dance. From what? For what? From corsets and shoes, Minkus and Delibes, pointes and port de bras? For Chopin waltzes, Wagner operas and Chaikovsky symphonies in bare feet and Greek tunics? If she was only a creator of styles in movement, music and dress, she was of minor importance and only indifferently successful, for all these innovations are already obsolete. In that case, let us proceed with the erection of the dolorous marble monument of prophecy, a sentimental monstrosity dictated by idolatry and memorialism and destined to make coming generations look on the legend of Isadora with something not far removed from contempt.

Instinctively one knows in the face of what has happened in the dance itself of recent years that such a theory is false, but rationally there is no specific body of facts to build upon. Only our temerarious scribe can supply the means for doing justice to an artist of epochal importance and what is more to the point, for protecting her magnificent heritage. No mere scholiast will serve, adding a timorous footnote here and an apologetic paraphrase there. It must be someone who will vigorously dispel the clouds, reduce what he finds beneath them to the simplest fundamental terms, and boldly fill what gaps he uncovers.

## II

Let us see, in broad outline, what his textbook must include.

In the first place, Isadora was not concerned with establishing a new school of dancing, called the Duncan Dance, or what you will. She was militantly opposed to schools, systems, and professionalism in general. What she was primarily concerned with can only be called basic dance—not a trade or a profession or even an art to begin with, but a biological function. She was not seeking to invent or devise anything, but only to discover the roots of that impulse toward movement as a response to every experience, which she felt in herself and which she was convinced was a universal endowment. Without benefit of formal psychology, she knew as no other dancer on record had known that spontaneous movement of the body is the first reaction of all men to sensory or emotional stimuli. Though civilization tends to dull and to inhibit this tendency, it is still the fundamental reaction of men to the universe about them.

3

Isadora Duncan. New York City. Schloss, 1898.

A revival of the conscious use of this faculty would mean deepening and broadening the whole range of life. If the individual becomes aware of the world in which he lives through its direct effect upon his nerves and muscles, nature's fundamental perceptive mechanism, he has won his freedom from the arbitrary thou-shalts and shalt-nots which established social cults and creeds put upon him the moment he is old enough to be dominated. Only when he has developed the power to touch life at first hand does he begin to be aware of his inherent selfhood, and until he has become thus aware he cannot develop his true bent or resist the forces that would conventionalize him into a mass product.

This was and is a colossal concept, not only affecting the dance but virtually adding another dimension to life. It plays havoc with categories, upsets tradition, destroys rote and official revelation. Yet its theory has been eloquently enunciated both in words

4

and in its own stuff of responsive movement by Isadora, it has been practiced by a generation of other dancers through a kind of subconscious transfer and advanced by them far beyond the rational grasp of its laws, and it is now quite possible for our textbook to present it in terms of a logical and workable technical procedure. All that is required, besides the qualities of insight, courage, and practicality already enumerated, is a thorough knowledge of anatomy, psychology, esthetics and education!

Isadora, however, without any scientific equipment whatever, has indicated all the true directions and many of the exact roads to be traveled. She has related how, once she had become convinced through her own experience that movement arose from a central inner source which she called the soul, she sought to find where in the body this source was located and how it was to be stirred to action. The word "soul" is likely to frighten us today, but if it is allowed to do so we will miss the whole point of Isadora's basic dance. For her it meant simply that correlative of the mind which produced, instead of intellectual concepts, quite irrational expressions of feeling. It was no more confined to a physical organ than the mind is confined to the brain, but she felt that it must have some correlative "habitation" in the body. For hours she stood before the mirror in a concentration that suggests the Orient, seeking this bodily center, and the conclusion of her quest was amazingly analytical. Through watching, apparently quite objectively, her emotional and motor impulses and relating them to each other, she discovered to her complete satisfaction that the solar plexus was the bodily habitation of the soul and the center in which inner impulse was translated into movement. If we are to take her literally at her word and accept the fact that by these solitary experiments she was able actually to isolate internal nervous experience in this way, it is one of the most astounding accomplishments on record. But even if she began with a considerable basis of theory, her discovery remains remarkable for its soundness in relating emotion to visceral action and visceral action to outward movement. She had, however crudely and in whatever inaccurate and unscientific terminology, discovered the soul to be what less imaginative men have called the autonomic system.

On this revolutionary principle she based all her practice and her teaching, and our textbook must do likewise until a greater researcher arises to supersede it. But a principle without a technique to make it operative is merely an abstraction, and here Isadora arrived at less tangible results. Her efforts, however, are a guide as well as a check upon more specific methods that may (and must) be devised by others.

How to start the motor in the soul, as she once phrased the impulsion to move? Her own chief means was music—Wagner, Beethoven, all the great romanticists of the nineteenth century—music which stirred the emotions; but she knew that this was not the solution and said so. Nor was this the only means she employed. She surrounded her young pupils with paintings and sculpture to form their standards of action visually, and she turned them to the processes of nature for the same end. Presumably besides listening to music "with the soul" they were to be guided subconsciously by the ideal of living beauty which was held before their eyes.

But most important of all her approaches to the subject were the experiments she made not with stimulation by other arts but directly with personal emotion. She has described her search for certain key movements which should arise out of elemental emotional experiences such as fear and love, and from which a whole series of developing movement should flow as of its own volition. These experiments were important for several reasons, but to the present topic they are of especial significance. She has told us nothing at all about her mode of procedure in these experiments, but it can easily be supplied from the context, and in it lies the answer to the problem. Here we find her deliberately invoking specific emotional states without music or any other external aid, and the only possible means that lay within herself was memory. In order to discover a "first movement" of fear from which a sequence of related and developing movements should proceed in natural order, a state resembling fear itself must be re-created to stimulate the impulses of suitable movement. This could only be done by recalling previous experiences of fear and allowing these memories freely to induce their own bodily and emotional states.

Isadora made use of certain actual phrases of movement discovered by these experiments, but she did not carry the method itself through to its full development, and missed accordingly the basic technical process of her art. A colleague, however, did carry it through in another art and for slightly different ends. This was Constantin

London. Dover Street Studios, 1910.

Stanislavsky of the Moscow Art Theater who demanded from his actors the same kind of emotional truth, arising from the same kind of inner impulsion, that Isadora demanded from herself and all dancers. His use of affective memory as the root of the actor's technique was more deliberate than Isadora's and consciously shaped into a clear-cut, teachable method for training actors.

To reconcile the differences between an actor's technique and a dancer's need is the first major task of our textbook. The actor, at least as Stanislavsky saw him, works in terms of naturalism, while the dancer, in Isadora's sense of the word, deals in great abstractions of human experience; but it is the same truth that underlies both their arts, for they are in essence only one art in different guises. Already, however, considerable experimentation has been done in adapting the principles of Stanislavsky to the problems of the dancer, and the textbook, therefore, need not be delayed for any prolonged research along uncharted ways. It is possible immediately to present an orderly method for starting Isadora's motor of the soul, avoiding all the pitfalls that threatened her and using ultimately the very principles that she found for herself without knowing she had done so. It need remain no longer a vague and inspirational process.

## III

But this is the beginning rather than the end of the problem. Even though it is possible to produce technically by the conscious use of affective processes motor reactions that are honest and true, it does not necessarily follow that dance movement has been produced. Dance movement is not a mere succession of motions, however inspired, but exists in terms of sustained dynamic tone, just as song is not a mere succession of sounds but exists in terms of sustained vocal tone.

It was music that supplied the necessary transforming element for Isadora. If it served first of all to lower the threshold of motor activation for her, it also provided a continuity of impulse. As long as its emotional qualities had power to stir her, she was provided with an impetus to evolve a continuum of movement, so to speak, of genuinely responsive character. She had learned to make herself so sensitive to this kind of impul-

Isadora Duncan. Munich. Elvira, 1902. (Courtesy Edwin Denby)

sion that she could sustain movement with unfaltering emotional truth through entire symphonies. It was only under this form of stimulation, she declared, that she was able to rediscover "the natural cadences of human movements," but obviously this did not satisfy her as a basic method, for instead of giving herself up to it indulgently and considering the matter closed, she set about searching for tangible, controllable technical means. Significantly enough, in the two important phases of this search—the location of the "central crater of motor power" and the evocation of "first movements"—she eschewed the use of music altogether.

It is these experiments in the production of "first movements" that must here concern us once more. In them she was aiming not merely at the production without external stimulation of creative motor responses, but at the production of motor responses each of which should result in a sequence of movement unfolding along the line of its specific

9

*La Marseillaise.* New York. Arnold Genthe, 1916.

emotional origin. Such a sequence implies inherent continuity of tone as well as progression in a consistent direction. It is a parallel in its own medium of the phrase in music and was probably being sought as such by Isadora. Certainly the example of music was not absent from her mind, for though she worked in silence she declared that these movements "seemed to create themselves from the rhythm of some invisible music." A sequence of movement flowing as if of its own volition from a single emotional impulse is actually a motor phrase, the lowest common denominator of dance movement and the basic unit of composition. It is the transformation of the simple feeling-acting technique, which produces individual expressive motions known as gestures, into the broader and more intensive stuff which we call movement and of which art is made.

Isadora apparently made no formal adaptation whatever of these extraordinary experiments to her teaching methods. There is an intuitive awareness of the character of the motor phrase, perhaps, in her insistence that the exercises of her young pupils always have an entity of their own and never lapse into isolated movements or mere muscular exertion. What she may have done in this field when she led her classes into improvisations it is impossible to tell, but certainly she left no definite instructions for teaching the individual discovery of "first movements" and the development of the motor phrase.

Again our pedagogue must turn to Stanislavsky for general guidance if not for specific instructions. The method of improvisation is undoubtedly indicated here; first, for the gradual strengthening of the ability to sustain emotion, and second, for the recognition of the natural tendency of emotion thus sustained to feed upon itself, resulting, almost literally of its own volition, in invention and perception that the individual is unaware of possessing. Stanislavsky's practices along these lines are helpful but too literal on the one hand and too diffuse on the other, for the dancer must concentrate his responses into the motor field exclusively and must lift them completely out of the category of merely expressive gesture. This is a by no means impossible transition, but it increases immeasurably the dangers, which already inhere in Stanislavsky's method, of auto-hypnosis and virtual nervous debauchery. It is extremely perilous ground on which our pedagogue treads here, and if he turns back fearing his responsibility, he need not consider himself cowardly. Many dancers have turned back here, for the work enters the rather despised field of pure self-expression, at best, and from there may easily wander off into pathological regions. If he is the true pedagogue that he must be to undertake such a textbook, however, he will know how to erect the necessary controls which the artist-dancer, who is not necessarily a pedagogue at all, will not know how to erect. Actual experimentation has already been done in the dance field which eliminates these hazards and the chief task in so far as the textbook is concerned is to reduce the experimentation to orderly principles and teachable practices. A delicate job, if you will, but a perfectly feasible one, and without it there is no earthly way of insuring the translation of inner emotional impulsion directly into the stuff of the dance.

## I V

Thus far the problem has been altogether a subcutaneous one, so to speak; but the instrument of the dance is the outward body, and its adjustment to the demands made upon it is quite as important as the demands themselves. The greatest potential singer in the world armed with the most magnificent songs can do nothing unless he has an adequate voice and complete control of it, and the dancer is in the same situation. He not only needs to know how to play his instrument, but he must also build it out of himself and keep it tuned at all times. It is not enough that the body which is his instrument is a healthy enough body to take him through his daily living without limitation or disturbance; the body of the dancer is no more the half-conscious vehicle that carries him about from home to business, fumbling with hats and coats, papers and carfare, than the singer's voice is the sound-making apparatus with which he orders his coffee and chats about the weather. The dancer's body is a totally sentient organism capable of encompassing movements far more extended in range and dynamism, speed, and elasticity, than those encountered in routine living. It makes no difference at all that in his dancing he is dealing with the impulses and experiences of nature, projecting only the passions of men, and not attempting acrobatic feats, contortions, or any movements that violate nature; he is nevertheless not dealing in naturalistic gestures and so-called life movements, for he is presenting an idealization, an interpretation, a concentration of life experience, which because it is less diffuse than actuality must be correspondingly more intense.

How, then, to prepare the body for this larger-than-life function? Isadora was convinced that some form of gymnastic training was necessary before dance training as such could begin, but she is not specific about what it should consist of. There are certain things, however, that she knew it should not consist of, and these help to clear the ground. First, it must not be mere muscle development. The dancer is not a professional strong man whose business it is to flex his biceps, lift weights, and put shot; neither his individual musculature nor his skills are ends in themselves and it is worse

Isadora and her husband, the Russian poet, Essenin. New York, 1922.

than useless to develop them as such. Worse because the body is a wonderfully efficient organism which, for the conservation of its energy, makes everything habitual as quickly as possible. In order to avoid sending every incoming impression through the whole taxing process of emotional awareness and conscious examination, it establishes short cuts at the first opportunity by which familiar stimuli can be shunted off immediately to familiar reactions practically automatically. Thus the exercises which through repetition enlarge muscles soon become associated with no other function, and result in movement that is emotionally barren and the very reverse of expressive. The dancer's habit of moving must be made such that movement is never an end in itself but always the outward result of an inward awareness.

It follows, then, that no series of set movements, whatever their virtues for muscle development, can be established as a training technique. It does not matter whether they are devised according to an impersonal, scientific plan, or are merely an adaptation of some individual artist's personal inspiration crystallized into a vocabulary. The dancer must be trained neither to make somebody else's movements nor to resort to mechanically contrived routines, but quite to the contrary every ounce of his energy must be directed to the task of moving in his own highly personal and essentially unique manner. Obviously, the exercises by which he builds his bodily technique must consist accordingly of movements drawn out of himself as responses to emotional stimuli, but calculated at the same time to extend his physical capacity along all the required gymnastic lines.

Isadora met this problem in a way that is certainly too simple for the wider field of today, but that is nevertheless indicative of her intentions and perhaps even of a line of practical development. Her exercises (and there is no indication that the gymnastics that she advocated as pre-dance training were given to her young pupils through any other channel) consisted of movement processes common to everybody in the round of ordinary experience—walking, running, skipping, leaping, and the like. In making use of these materials she was assuredly putting nothing arbitrary or external upon the pupils, but was taking advantage of natural and, indeed, inevitable motor patterns of their own as a basis for operation. Though they were far too habitual even in young children to be considered as inherently creative movement, she actually reoriented them so that they were in large measure creatively produced. Whether or not this was possible with any but young children, or even invariably with them, is open to question, but it was definitely accomplished in many cases. To see such elementary movements as these performed in this way is to realize how little elaboration and extravagance of movement are necessary to command attention, to achieve a transfer of emotional experience and to provide genuine artistic satisfaction, when there is a complete unison of inward prompting and outward manifestation.

Because Isadora's dance was simple in its gymnastic demands, she was undoubtedly able to develop all the needed strength, elasticity and endurance under cover of these natural movements. But for increased requirements along these lines, her method (or at least this aspect of it) remains substantially sound with only a corresponding increase in dimensions. Actually the different types of movement of which the body is capable are remarkably few; tension and relaxation, flexion and extension, rotation, torsion and transfer of weight come pretty close to covering the entire range in broad terms. If our inspired pedagogue will only devise themes for improvisation with emotional demands designed explicitly to result in each of these necessary elements of movement and to bring into play in turn and in conjunction the various parts of the body, he can succeed in his more intensive medium as Isadora succeeded in her simple one. If he is really qualified to prepare this exemplary textbook, he can evolve a thorough and practicable method for the vigorous technical training of the dancer's body without resorting to a single superimposed routine or a solitary example of formal gymnastics. He will not, perhaps, produce acrobats thus, but he will produce dancers, provided always that he has talent to work with.


V


Another element in this pre-dance gymnastic training has to do with guarding the individuality of every dancer's style of movement. Isadora's use of natural movement for training purposes at least recognized the existence of the problem, but did not attempt to solve it, at its source. It is all very well to call walking, running and skipping natural, but they are natural to the race rather than to the individual. Every individual will walk and run differently according to his bodily formations and those less tangible aspects of his personality which we call his temperament; what then is the natural way to walk? Is there some ideal racial norm that must be discovered and imitated? If so, is this natural to the individual who, left to his own devices, will behave otherwise? If not, is whatever way the individual happens to walk natural to him even if it is perhaps caused by some muscular or nervous abnormality? Is deformity or eccentricity the same thing as individuality? If so, might it not be the better part of wisdom just to forget all about preserving individuality and begin superimposing harmonious routines that will obscure it?

If we are to encourage the individual to move according to his particular endowments, it is incumbent upon us at the same time not to encourage him to emphasize his weaknesses to his ultimate destruction. First, obviously, we must help him to establish his norm. This will involve consideration of basic body mechanics, the correction of postural misalignments and the removal of the psychic disturbances of which they are frequently the result. Here, again, our erudite pedagogue will have to call in an expert, for he has found the juncture of the dance with therapy of a closely related type. Much of the work will be done by methods curiously akin to that which lies at the center of Isadora's theory, for in making these postural and mechanical adjustments in the body, the most advanced practice makes use of mental imagery to produce reactions in deep muscles that are not under voluntary control. However, our textbook, being thorough and consistent, will inevitably demand not only theoretical quotations but also personal tuition from a "body mechanician"—a Mabel Elsworth Todd, for example, or a Lulu Sweigard or a Margaret Paulding, who stem from her teaching directly or indirectly —both for the establishment of the individual norm in the first place and for frequent periodic checks to make sure that it is being maintained. Until some such practice is instituted, talking about natural movement and the preservation of individuality is just so much loose and romantic verbiage. And that is exactly the stuff that our whole project is designed to destroy.

## VI

Here, perhaps, would end the first volume of the textbook. By means strictly in accord with Isadora's theory but employing the best contemporary technical developments, it has produced a dancer. There is much more, indeed, to be treated of from the same source and in the same manner before the subject is finished. The dancer, once produced, must learn to compose his dances, to choose his music, to design his costumes, and the basis of his procedure is admirably set forth in principle in Isadora's essays and autobiography. For all the Pre-Raphaelite sense of beauty that is commonly attributed to her, she has argued eloquently for what is sometimes called ugliness, and her method of evolving form out of content is worthy of the deepest study; her restoration of the body from exile is still not understood or practiced as it should be; and even in her attitude to music, the least amenable of her theories, there are pregnant hints about modern music and the future in general.

Our newly made dancer must have an insight into the rather profound esthetics of his great preceptor in order to allow her to lead him into paths which she herself never traveled. He will discover, for one thing, that her dance was lyric because all art is lyric in the beginning. The artist first gives expression to his personal emotions, even though he may couch them in heroic and impersonal terms. (Isadora "never once danced a solo," but "tried always to be the Chorus.") Next he materializes a protagonist, a concentrated figure who dances with the chorus; and finally an antagonist emerges as well—and the theater is born. The lyric base has not been destroyed but augmented, and the contemporary trend of the dance toward the theater can find orderly principles for its procedure in Isadora's lyric precedent.

All that, however, is for Volume Two.

Isadora in *La Primavera*. Paris, ca. 1900.

# Duncan Concerts in New York

## BY CARL VAN VECHTEN

*November 10, 1909*

Miss Isadora Duncan, who has evolved a style of choreographic art which corresponds in a measure at least—according to a comparison with the figures on ancient vases—with the dances of the ancient Greeks, made her reappearance in New York last evening at the Metropolitan Opera House, assisted by Walter Damrosch and the New York Symphony Orchestra.

The program stated that Miss Duncan would dance to the ballets and choruses of *Gluck's Iphigénie en Aulide.* Most of her dances were accomplished to such aid, but at least one of them, a Chorus of Priestesses, was taken from *Iphigénie en Tauride,* and its original purpose and signification were greatly distorted by the dancer. It is a number which was never designed for dancing, and to anyone who has heard it in its proper place in the opera it must seem more or less of a sacrilege to have it put to such purpose.

There can be no possible objection, however, to Miss Duncan's appropriating the ballet numbers from the Gluck operas for her particular purpose. It is a well-known fact that Gluck composed many of his ballets because they were demanded by the audiences of his time rather than by the exigencies of his operas. It is also quite as true that the list of them includes much that is best of the Gluck music.

They are particularly fitted in their nobility and lack of sensuousness to accompany the moods and poses which Miss Duncan portrays in her dances. She is at her best in dances which depict life and gaiety and motion. In this she is always sure of communicating her meaning to an audience. The Bacchanale which ended the formal program exhibited her finest talents. The play of the arms in the moderato and allegro in which the Maidens of Chalkis play at ball and knuckle bones by the seashore was also one of the effective bits.

The dances last night were in nowise different from those in which Miss Duncan has appeared in past seasons in this country and Europe, and her draperies were the same beautiful Greek arrangements. Repetitions of several of the dances were demanded by the large audience, and at the end of the program Miss Duncan added several extra numbers, concluding with *The Beautiful Blue Danube* waltz.

### November 17, 1909

Miss Isadora Duncan again appeared at the Metropolitan Opera House yesterday afternoon and danced for the first time this season to Beethoven's A major symphony, which was played by the New York Symphony Orchestra, with Walter Damrosch conducting. It is quite within the province of the recorder of musical affairs to protest against this perverted use of the Seventh Symphony, a purpose which Beethoven certainly never had in mind when he wrote it. Because Wagner dubbed it the "apotheosis of the dance" is not sufficient reason why it should be danced to.

However, if one takes it for granted that Miss Duncan has a right to perform her dances to whatever music she chooses, there is no doubt of the high effect she achieves. Seldom has she been more poetical, more vivid in her expression of joy, more plastic in her poses, more rhythmical in her effects than she was yesterday. Wagner's title for the symphony might very properly be applied to Miss Duncan. As usual, she was most effective in the dances which require decisive movement. One of the wildest of her dances she closed with arms outstretched and head thrown back almost out of sight until she resembled the headless Nike of Samothrace.

The orchestra played Chaikovsky's *Marche Slave*, a pantomime from Mozart's ballet music to *Les Petits Riens*, and a Beethoven *Polonaise* for the second part of the program and then Miss Duncan danced five Chopin numbers. The audience was large and enthusiastic.

*February 16, 1911*

Miss Isadora Duncan, the American girl who is directly responsible for a train of barefoot dancers who have spread themselves, like a craze, over two continents in the last five years, has returned to America, and yesterday she gave a new exhibition of her dancing, with the assistance of Walter Damrosch and the Symphony Society, at Carnegie Hall. Before the doors opened there were no seats to be had, and the long line of carriages which drew nigh the portals, as the hour set for the dancing to begin approached, indicated that Miss Duncan not only was the first of the barefoot dancers, but also the last. She not only has established her vogue, but she has also maintained it.

It has long been the custom for Miss Duncan to dance to music which originally belonged either to the opera house or the concert room. In years gone by she has lifted her feet to Chopin measures; to dances from the Gluck operas; and even to Beethoven's Seventh Symphony. This last was considered by many as a desecrating escapade, but many others paid money to see her do it, and Miss Duncan achieved some of her greatest popular success with the symphony which Wagner called the "apotheosis of the dance." Doubtless many people thereby became acquainted with a work of Beethoven which they never would have heard otherwise.

Yesterday Miss Duncan forsook the masters who have given her most of her material for dancing until now. She had arranged, in fact, an entirely new program, through which to display her art. It was made up of excerpts from the Wagner music dramas and Bach's *Suite in D.*

If Bach did not intend that his music should be danced to, at least several of the numbers in this suite bear the names of dances, so Miss Duncan cannot be taken too much to task for employing them for her purposes.

The stage setting was what it usually is at a Duncan séance. Green curtains depended from the heights of the stage and fell in folds at the back and sides leaving a semi-circular floor in the center on which dim rose-colored lights flitted here, contrasting with shadows there. When Mr. Damrosch came to the conductor's desk and raised his baton, all the lights in the auditorium were extinguished. The orchestra played the prelude to the suite and then Miss Duncan appeared.

Autograph photo for Mary Fanton Roberts, ca. 1911. (Courtesy M. F. Roberts)

She wore, as she always does, some drapery of diaphanous material. She stood for a moment in the shadow at the back of the stage while the orchestra began the *Air*, the celebrated slow movement in the suite, which violinists play on the G string. Miss Duncan waved her arms and posed during this movement but did not do much of what is conventionally called dancing.

In the two Gavottes and the Gigue which followed, however, the dancer was seen at her best. She flitted about the stage in her early Greek way and gave vivid imitations of what one may see on the spherical bodies of Greek vases. The Bourée from the suite the orchestra played alone and the first part of the program closed with the Polacca from the first *Brandenburg Concerto*, also undanced.

There was a brief intermission before the Wagner excerpts were played. Then the house was darkened and the *Lohengrin* Prelude was performed. After this Miss Duncan gave her interpretation of the Flower Maidens' music from *Parsifal*.

This time she appeared in white gauze, beautifully draped. Her hair was caught up with flowers of pinkish hue. She evidently danced with an imaginary "Guileless Fool" standing in the center of the stage. To him she appealed with all her gestures and all her postures. It was an interesting attempt to give the spirit of the scene in the Klingsor's garden. What it meant to those who have never heard Wagner's music drama this writer cannot profess to know.

The next number announced on the program was the Prelude and *Liebestod* from *Tristan und Isolde*. Instead, however, of rapping for attention from his orchestra, Mr. Damrosch asked the audience for attention, turned about, and made a little speech.

The purport of his remarks was to the effect that it had originally been intended that Miss Duncan dance only music which had been arranged by Wagner in his music dramas for that purpose.

"It had been my intention," said Mr. Damrosch, "simply to play this music from *Tristan*. Yesterday, however, Miss Duncan modestly asked me if I would go through the *Liebestod* with her. She has, as is well known, a desire to unite dancing to music in a perfect whole, as an art which existed in the time of the early Greeks. Whatever she does now, of course, must be largely experimental. However, the results which she has already achieved with the *Liebestod* are so interesting that I think it only fair to set them before the public. As there are probably a great many people here to whom the idea of giving pantomimic expression to the *Liebestod* would be horrifying, I am putting it last on the program, so that those who do not wish to see it may leave."

There was applause and then Miss Duncan gave her impressions of the Paris version of the Bacchanale from *Tannhäuser,* which were very pretty but hardly as bacchanalian as might have been expected. After the orchestra had played the Prelude to *Die Meister-singer* she danced the Dance of the Apprentices from that music drama. It may be stated that Miss Duncan did her best dancing of the afternoon to this number and it was repeated.

As for the *Liebestod,* the anticipation of it evidently was not too horrible for anyone to bear. People did not leave their seats, except possibly the usual few who are obliged to catch trains. Miss Duncan's conception of the music did not seem to suggest a pantomimic Isolde, nor was it exactly dancing. In other words, she puzzled those who knew the music drama, and did not interest those who did not. Therefore one may ask, Why?

*February 21, 1911*

It was to the operas of Gluck that Miss Isadora Duncan went for her first inspiration when she began her revivals of the Greek dance, and yesterday afternoon in Carnegie Hall she returned to Gluck. Her previous attempt to dance to the music from the lyric dramas of Richard Wagner had not resulted in complete success, but her spectators yesterday were pleased to see that Miss Duncan was herself again.

The first half of the program consisted of copious excerpts from *Orfeo,* played in chronological order, and embracing the chief incidents of the book, with the exception of the scene in which Eurydice persuades Orpheus to turn and gaze upon her face. The Symphony Society of New York, Walter Damrosch conducting, played the music; a small chorus, seated among the orchestra, sang several of the choruses, and Mme. Florence Mulford sang several of Orpheus's airs.

In the first act, in a long robe of flowing gray, Miss Duncan represented one of the companions of Orpheus. Her poses and movements were intended to suggest the deepest grief. It was in the first scene of the second act, that of the scene in Hades, which was given in its entirety, that Miss Duncan, portraying one of the Furies, first aroused the enthusiasm of the audience. She indicated the gradual wavering of the Furies from the tremendous "No" in the beginning to the end when the Furies allow Orpheus to pass on to the Elysian Fields. The Dance of the Furies, with which this scene concludes, was a remarkable exhibition of dancing, evidence of high imagination.

It had originally been intended that several of the choruses and Orpheus's air from the scene of the Elysian Fields should be included in the program scheme, but evidently it was found necessary to omit these. Only the ballet airs were presented from this scene, including the famous air with flute obbligato, which was exquisitely played by Mr. Barrère.

Miss Duncan, as a Happy Spirit, was as much at home as she had been previously as a Fury. From here on a long excision was made in the score until the finale was reached; even the famous chaconne was omitted. In the final scene, in which the chorus again appeared, Miss Duncan indicated the triumph of Love.

The excerpts were beautifully played by Mr. Damrosch and his orchestra. It is worthy of note that the seldom heard overture, a usually omitted ballet air, and the finale, which is replaced at the Metropolitan Opera House by a finale from another opera of Gluck, were restored. As has been stated, much else was omitted.

After an intermission Miss Duncan danced to some music by Schubert, and the orchestra played Dvořák's *In the Spinning Room.*

At the Parthenon, 1920. Writing in her autobiography *My Life*, Isadora reports: "The painter Edward Steichen who was one of our party took many lovely pictures in the Acropolis and in the theatre of Dionysius which faintly foreshadowed the splendid vision I longed to create in Greece."

# The New Isadora

## BY CARL VAN VECHTEN

I HAVE a fine memory of a chance description flung off by someone at a dinner in Paris; a picture of the youthful Isadora Duncan in her studio in New York developing her ideals through sheer will and preserving the contour of her feet by wearing carpet slippers. The latter detail stuck in my memory. It may or may not be true, but it could have been, *should* have been true. The incipient dancer keeping her feet pure for her coming marriage with her art is a subject for philosophic dissertation or for poetry. There are many poets who would have seized on this idea for an ode or even a sonnet, had it occurred to them. Oscar Wilde would have liked this excuse for a poem . . . even Robert Browning, who would have woven many moral strophes from this text. . . . It would have furnished Mr. George Moore with material for another story of the volume called *Celibates*. Walter Pater might have dived into some very beautiful, but very conscious, prose with this theme as a spring-board. Huysmans would have found this suggestion sufficient inspiration for a romance the length of *Clarissa Harlowe*. You will remember that the author of *En Route* meditated writing a novel about a man who left his house to go to his office. Perceiving that his shoes have not been polished, he stops at a boot-black's and during the operation he reviews his affairs. The problem was to make 300 pages of this! . . . Lombroso would have added the detail to his long catalogue in *The Man of Genius* as another proof of the insanity of artists. Georges Feydeau would have found therein enough matter for a three-act farce and d'Annunzio for a poetic drama which he might have dedicated to "Isadora of the beautiful feet."

Sermons might be preached from the text and many painters would touch the subject with reverence. Manet might have painted Isadora with one of the carpet slippers half depending from a bare, rosy-white foot.

There are many fables concerning the beginning of Isadora's career. One has it that the original dance in bare feet was an accident. . . . Isadora was laving her feet in an upper chamber when her hostess begged her to dance for her other guests. Just as she was she descended and met with such approval that thenceforth her feet remained bare. This is a pretty tale, but it has not the fine ring of truth of the story of the carpet slippers. There had been barefoot dancers before Isadora; there had been, I venture to say, distinct "Greek dancers." Isadora's contribution to her art is spiritual; it is her feeling for the idea of the dance which isolates her from her contemporaries. Many have overlooked this essential fact in attempting to account for her obvious importance. Her imitators (and has any other interpretative artist ever had so many?) have purloined her costumes, her gestures, her steps; they have put the music of Beethoven and Schubert to new uses as she had done before them; they have unbound their hair and freed their feet; but the essence of her art, the spirit, they have left in her keeping; they could not well do otherwise.

Inspired perhaps by Greek phrases, by the superb collection of Greek vases in the old Pinakothek in Munich, Isadora cast the knowledge she had gleaned of the dancer's training from her. At least she forced it to be subservient to her new wishes. She flung aside her memory of the *entrechat* and the *pirouette*, the studied technique of the ballet; but in so doing she unveiled her own soul. She called her art the renaissance of the Greek ideal but there was something modern about it, pagan though it might be in quality. Always it was pure and sexless . . . always abstract emotion has guided her interpretations.

In the beginning she danced to the piano music of Chopin and Schubert. Eleven years ago I saw her in Munich in a program of Schubert impromptus and Chopin preludes and mazurkas. A year or two later she was dancing in Paris to the accompaniment of the Colonne Orchestra, a good deal of the music of Gluck's *Orfeo* and the very lovely dances from *Iphigénie en Aulide*. In these she remained faithful to her original

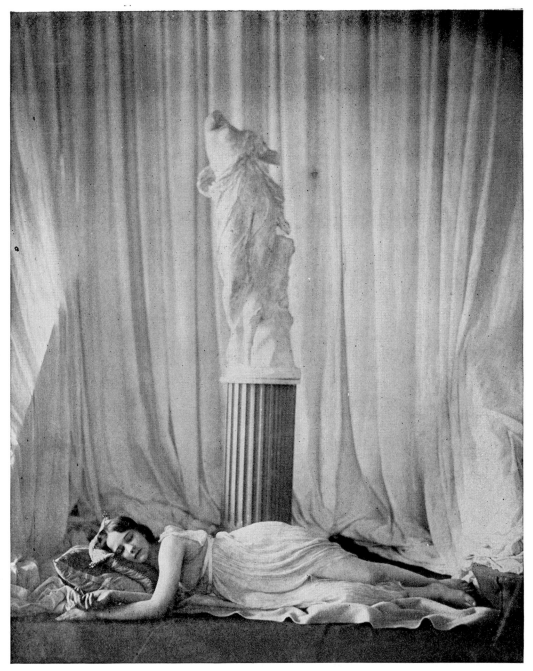

The Isadora Duncan Studio at Nice, ca. 1926.

ideal, the beauty of abstract movement, the rhythm of exquisite gesture. This was not sense echoing sound but rather a very delightful confusion of her own mood with that of the music.

So a new grace, a new freedom were added to the dance; in her later representations she has added a third quality, strength. Too, her immediate interpretations often suggest concrete images. . . . A passionate patriotism for one of her adopted countries is at the root of her fiery miming of the *Marseillaise*, a patriotism apparently as deep-rooted, certainly as inflaming, as that which inspired Rachel in her recitation of this hymn during the Paris revolution of 1848. In times of civil or international conflagration the dancer, the actress often play important roles in world politics. Malvina Cavalazzi, the Italian ballerina who appeared at the Academy of Music during the Eighties and who married Charles Mapleson, son of the impresario, once told me of a part she had played in the making of United Italy. During the Austrian invasion the Italian flag was *verboten*. One night, however, during a representation of opera in a town the name of which I have forgotten, Mme. Cavalazzi wore a costume of green and white, while her male companion wore red, so that in the *pas de deux* which concluded the ballet they formed automatically a semblance of the Italian banner. The audience was raised to a hysterical pitch of enthusiasm and rushed from the theater in a violent mood, which resulted in an immediate encounter with the Austrians and their eventual expulsion from the city.

Isadora's pantomimic interpretation of the *Marseillaise*, given in New York before the United States had entered the World War, aroused as vehement and excited an expression of enthusiasm as it would be possible for an artist to awaken in our theater today. The audience stood up and scarcely restrained their impatience to cheer. At the previous performances in Paris, I am told, the effect approached the incredible. . . . In a robe the color of blood she stands enfolded; she sees the enemy advance; she feels the enemy as it grasps her by the throat; she kisses her flag; she tastes blood; she is all but crushed under the weight of the attack; and then she rises, triumphant, with the terrible cry, *Aux armes, citoyens!* Part of her effect is gained by gesture, part by the massing of her body, but the greater part by facial expression. In the anguished appeal she does not make a sound, beyond that made by the orchestra, but the hideous din of a hundred raucous voices seems to ring in our ears. We see Félicien Rops's "Vengeance" come to life; we see the *sans-culottes* following the carts of the aristocrats on the way to execution . . . and finally we see the superb calm, the majestic flowing strength of the Victory of Samothrace. . . . At times, legs, arms, a leg or an arm, the throat, or the exposed breast assume an importance above that of the rest of the mass, suggesting the unfinished sculpture of Michael Angelo, an aposiopesis which, of course, served as Rodin's inspiration.

In the *Marche Slave* of Chaikovsky Isadora symbolizes her conception of the Russian moujik rising from slavery to freedom. With her hands bound behind her back, groping, stumbling, head bowed, knees bent, she struggles forward, clad only in a short red garment that barely covers her thighs. With furtive glances of extreme despair she peers above and ahead. When the strains of *God Save the Czar* are first heard in the orchestra she falls to her knees and you see the peasant shuddering under the blows of the knout. The picture is a tragic one, cumulative in its horrific details. Finally comes the moment of release and here Isadora makes one of her great effects. She does not spread her arms apart with a wide gesture. She brings them forward slowly and we observe with horror that they have practically forgotten how to move at all. They are crushed, these hands, crushed and bleeding after their long serfdom; they are not hands at all but claws, broken, twisted piteous claws! The expression of frightened, almost uncomprehending, joy with which Isadora concludes the march is another stroke of her vivid imaginative genius.

In her third number inspired by the Great War, the *Marche Lorraine* of Louis Ganne, in which is incorporated the celebrated *Chanson Lorraine*, Isadora with her pupils, symbolizes the gaiety of the martial spirit. It is the spirit of the cavalry riding gallantly with banners waving in the wind; the infantry marching to an inspired tune. There is nothing of the horror of war or revolution in this picture . . . only the brilliancy and dash of war . . . the power and the glory!

Of late years Isadora has danced (in the conventional meaning of the word) less and less. Since her performance at Carnegie Hall several years ago of the *Liebestod* from

*Tristan*, which Walter Damrosch hailed as an extremely interesting experiment, she has attempted to express something more than the joy of melody and rhythm. Indeed on at least three occasions she has performed a Requiem at the Metropolitan Opera House. . . . If the new art at its best is not dancing, neither is it wholly allied to the art of pantomime. It would seem, indeed, that Isadora is attempting to express something of the spirit of sculpture, perhaps what Vachel Lindsay describes as "moving sculpture." Her medium, of necessity, is still rhythmic gesture, but its development seems almost dreamlike. More than the dance this new art partakes of the fluid and unending quality of music. Like any other new art it is not to be understood at first and I confess in the beginning it said nothing to me, but eventually I began to take pleasure in watching it. Now Isadora's poetic and imaginative interpretation of the symphonic interlude from César Franck's *Rédemption* is full of beauty and meaning to me and during the whole course of its performance the interpreter scarcely rises from her knees. The neck, the throat, the shoulders, the head and arms are her means of expression. I thought of Barbey d'Aurevilly's, *"Elle avait l'air de monter vers Dieu les mains toutes pleines de bonnes œuvres."*

Isadora's teaching has had its results but her influence has been wider in other directions. Fokine thanks her for the new Russian Ballet. She did indeed free the Russians from the conventions of the classic ballet and but for her it is doubtful if we should have seen *Scheherazade* and *Cléopâtre*. *Daphnis et Chloë*, *Narcisse* and *l'Après-midi d'un Faune* bear her direct stamp. This then, aside from her own appearances, has been her great work. Of her celebrated school of dancing I cannot speak with so much enthusiasm. The defect in her method of teaching is her insistence (consciously or unconsciously) on herself as a model. The seven remaining girls of her school dance delightfully. They are, in addition, young and beautiful, but they are miniature Isadoras. They add nothing to her style; they make the same gestures; they take the same steps; they have almost, if not quite, acquired a semblance of her spirit. They vibrate with intention; they have force, but constantly they suggest just what they are . . . imitations. When they dance alone they often make a very charming but scarcely overpowering effect. When they dance with Isadora they are but a moving row of shadow shapes of Isadora that come and go. Her own presence suffices to make the effect they all make together. . . . I have been told that when Isadora watches her girls dance she often weeps, for then and then only she can behold herself. One of the griefs of an actor or a dancer is that he can never see himself. This oversight of nature Isadora has to some extent overcome.

Those who like to see pretty dancing, pretty girls, pretty things in general will not find much pleasure in contemplating the art of Isadora. She is not pretty; her dancing is not pretty. She has been cast in nobler mold and it is her pleasure to climb higher mountains. Her gesture is titanic; her mood generally one of imperious grandeur. She has grown larger with the years—and by this I mean something more than the physical interpretation of the word, for she is indeed heroic in build. But this is the secret of her power and force. There is no suggestion of flabbiness about her and so she can impart to us the soul of the struggling moujik, the spirit of a nation, the figure on the prow of a Greek bark. . . . And when she interprets the *Marseillaise* she seems indeed to feel the mighty moment.

*July 14, 1917*

Water color and pencil drawing. Auguste Rodin. Paris, ca. 1906.

34

# Isadora Duncan and the Artists

## BY ALLAN ROSS MACDOUGALL

AT VARIOUS TIMES during her later years, Isadora Duncan was heard to say, when questioned about the genesis of her dance: "I sprang full-fledged from the head of Zeus!" We who knew and loved her never quite dared challenge the dogmatic statement, although we knew that her art, like many such manifestations of genius, was a rare plant of slow and continual growth. We knew, and of course Isadora also knew, that the final, full flowering of her dance bore slight semblance of relation to the first wrinkled seed planted within her, who knows how or when.

Through the years the seed was watered by many rains and its first frail sprout warmed by many suns. The growth of the plant was nurtured and encouraged by many outside influences; occasionally it was pruned by self-criticism. Whatever dancing the young Californian did in her childhood days in San Francisco and her early travels across the continent to New York, certainly bore no relation to that exhibited at her tremendous final performance in Paris in 1927, the 49th year of her life. The innocuous little pieces mimed with Delsartean gestures to music by Ethelbert Nevin and the lesser Romantic composers, were childish, fumbling, clay-modeled figurines compared to the heroic, the monumental works such as César Franck's *Rédemption*, or the *Tannhäuser Overture* and *Bacchanale*, which were only part of that last performance at the Mogador Theater.

In her early days Isadora's dance was always referred to as *Greek*. This, doubtless, because she adopted flowing Greek draperies and performed her dance with feet and

35

Isadora Duncan. Pastel drawing by Fritz von Kaulbach. Munich, 1902. (Used as a cover for the magazine *Jugend*, 1904.)

arms bare; she also confessed quite frankly that she studied Hellenic sculpture and vase paintings.

"During my youth," she once wrote to the editor of the French daily, *Progrès d'Athènes*, "I spent long hours of admiring enthusiasm before the Parthenon and its friezes, the frescoes, the Greek vases, the Tanagras, not with the idea of copying them or their attitudes, or the divine expression of these masterpieces, but really, after studying them at length, to try and get right to the depths of their primordial being and to attempt to discover the 'secret' of their ecstasy through spiritual exploration of the symbolic ideas of their gestures. From their mystery came my dance—not Greek, not Antique, but in reality the expression of my soul moved to harmony by Beauty."

From photographs it can be seen that in the '90's Isadora neither dressed *à la Grec* nor skipped about with unshod feet. Certain studio photographs taken in 1898 in New York, show the 20-year-old dancer wearing ballet slippers and a dress fashioned of lace. According to all accounts it was not until she had reached Europe and had met and been influenced by the English Philhellenes and the artists of Paris, that her dance became "free." The tentative shoot from the wrinkled seed began to open out, drinking in with avidity the warmth of the new climate of art and appreciation to which it had been transplanted.

If in her later years Isadora gave much to painters and sculptors so that she became, without any doubt, the most portrayed woman in the world, it is certain that in these early years at the turn of the century, she also received much inspiration and unspoken direction from artists with whom she associated. And together with the marvelous Greek collections of the British Museum and the Musée du Louvre, William Blake also contributed his share of inspiration and direction. I used to own, until some bibliophilic pilferer purloined it from Djuna Barnes to whom I had lent it, the dancer's copy of the Gilchrist *Life of Blake*. The copious marginal notes in the handwritings of Isadora and of Gordon Craig attested to a diligent study, not only of the text but also of the illustrations.

Isadora's own story of her brief career in England where she gave what, for want of a better phrase, is called "drawing-room entertainments," in the London houses of the gentry, and danced the First Fairy and other minor choreographic roles with the traveling Shakespearean company of the late Frank Benson, has been told in her autobiography. The English experience was merely a repetition, with cultural differences, of her life and art in New York, even down to her theatrical essays in dancing.

The turning point of Isadora's career as a dancer was undoubtedly her first visit in the year 1900 to Paris, the supreme capital of European art and culture. Then it was that she spent long hours and many days studying the Greek vases in the Louvre. With her brother Raymond—a gaunt young man who had not yet adopted his quasi-Greek get-up of hand-woven chiton and chlamys and hand-tooled sandals—the young visitor made the rounds of all the museums and monuments of the City of Light. "There was

**Isadora Duncan's Berliner Tanzschule**

Berlin, 1904. Caricature from the magazine *Jugend*. "In this period we shall finish with Mr. Beethoven. In the next we shall begin on Mr. Aeschylus." "Leave that alone Frau Duncan, and teach us Mr. Richsdorfer instead." (Richsdorfer was the name of a popular ragtime dance, taken from a Berlin suburb.)

not a monument," she later said, "before which we did not stand in adoration, our young American souls uplifted before this culture which we had striven so hard to find."

It was in that fateful year of 1900, at the exciting Exposition Universelle, that Isadora felt the tremendous impact of the double-barreled revelation of the marble and bronze of Auguste Rodin and the great tragic dancing of the Japanese artist Sada Yacco. These two experiences left indelible impressions on her sensitive mind. And with the youthful Californian intensity with which she was pursuing culture, Isadora and her English companion, Charles Halle, visited the Rodin Pavilion innumerable times, and night after night sat through the performances of "the wondrous art" of the famous Oriental dancer.

Through a nephew of Halle, Isadora was introduced into the world of art and artists after having been presented to Madame de St. Marceau at whose salon she danced one evening. Then followed a series of recitals given in various fashionable salons frequented by members of the French aristocracy and the reigning figures of the musical, artistic, and literary worlds—André Messager, André Beaunier, Jean Lorrain, Henri Bataille, the Comtesse de Noailles, Madeleine Lemaire, the Prince and Princesse Edmond de Polignac, and Eugène Carrière, to mention only a few of the better known names.

With the latter great artist, the American dancer became quite intimate. She was introduced into his humble and affectionate family circle. He painted her portrait in his monochromatic, vaporous style, a wholly different Isadora and completely divorced from the dancing figure portrayed so many times by other artists. Later in her more affluent days she bought two of Carrière's canvases which she always treasured and which she finally parted with under the stress of extreme poverty. So delighted was the paternal Carrière with her dancing that he prepared notes for a brief *causerie* which he delivered before one of her performances in a Paris salon, sometime in 1901.

"Isadora, wishing to express emotions," he wrote, "discovered in Greek art her finest models. Full of admiration for the lovely figures of the bas-reliefs, she adopted them as her inspiration. Yet, endowed with the instinct of discovery, she returned to Nature from whence came all these gestures, and thinking to imitate and give rebirth to Greek

Crayon drawing by Leon Bakst. Russia, 1908.

Portrait in oils by Eugène Carrière. Paris, ca. 1909.

Pen drawings of Isadora by Jean-Paul Lafitte. Paris, ca. 1909.

dancing, she found her own expression. She thinks of the Greeks and obeys but herself; she offers us her own joy and her own grief. In demonstrating to us her fine feelings so beautifully, she evokes ours: as before Greek statues revivified a moment for us, we are young again with her and a new hope triumphs within us. And when she expresses her resignation to the inevitable we also resign ourselves.

"Isadora Duncan's dance is no longer an entertaining diversion; it is a personal manifestation as well as a work of art, livelier and more fecund as an incentive to works which we ourselves are destined to do."

From this fruitful period in Paris dates not only the dancer's acquaintance with Rodin's work but also with the artist himself. Having admired almost daily his statues shown in the Rodin Pavilion at the Exposition, she finally made her way to the master's studio. This first meeting ripened into a very real mutual friendship and admiration for each other's art. Like the gentle and humble Carrière, the genial sculptor had a decided influence upon the young dancer. Later she was to rent one of the studios near him in the disused convent building, rue de l'Université, where Rodin created some of his noblest works.

In the year 1903, to celebrate Rodin's promotion to the rank of Commander of the Legion of Honor, a group of his pupils and intimate friends—among them Besnard, the distinguished painter, the sculptor Bourdelle, Octave Mirbeau, Fritz von Thaulow, and some others less well-known then—arranged an *al fresco* party at Vélizy, near Chaville, on the outskirts of Paris. Impromptu speeches were made and von Thaulow played his violin. Then, according to Frederick Lawton, who in 1907 wrote the first biography of the French master:

"Miss Isidora [sic] Duncan, an American lady, known in Paris for her rhythmic interpretations of Beethoven's music, rose and danced on the greensward, resuscitating as far as might be the terpsichorean art of old."

Here the stodgy Victorian biographer is less enthusiastic than his subject. For Rodin publicly expressed his whole-hearted appreciation of the art of the new dancer. He also made rapid sketches of her as she danced at various times. "It can be said of Isadora," he wrote, "that she has attained sculpture and emotion effortlessly. She has borrowed from Nature that force which cannot be called Talent but which is Genius.

"Miss Duncan has properly unified Life and the Dance. She is natural on the stage where people rarely are so. She makes her dance sensitive to line and is as simple as the Antiquity synonymous with Beauty. Suppleness, emotion, these high qualities which are the soul of the dance, are her complete and sovereign art."

The studies Rodin made of the dancer, like his equally well-known series of the Cambodian dancers, were rapid, calligraphic sketches, retouched with a thin, water-color wash. They are interesting, of course, and highly personal, but lack the precision of the younger Bourdelle's innumerable sketches of the dancer, or even those done by a sculptor of lesser fame, José Clara.

This young Catalan was one of an enthusiastic band of artists who attended en masse the first public performances given by Isadora in Paris. I recall his telling me that for the first performance, fearing the hall might not be filled, Raymond and Isadora appeared at the Ecole des Beaux-Arts and distributed to the astonished students, *billets de faveur*—or Annie Oakleys as Broadway jargon has it.

At these early recitals the young art students were the most vocal and zealous of the American dancer's admirers. With *sous* rashly subtracted from their meager allowances they would buy flowers at the dawn flowermarket in Les Halles, later to toss them at their idol's feet. In happy, noisy bands they would mob the stage doors of the Châtelet or the Gaîté theaters, where Lugné-Poé, later to become famous as an actor-manager at the Théâtre de L'Œuvre but then acting as manager for Isadora, would finally say: "*Vous, les étudiants, vous pouvez entrer.*" And often, according to my informant, when the announced program had terminated, Isadora would step to the front of the stage and say in her quaintly accented French: "*Je vais danser encore une danse pour mes amis, les étudiants des Beaux-Arts,*" embracing in that appellation all the enthusiastic spectators of the upper balconies.

As is customary among French art students, most of these budding artists brought their sketch books to the theater and found in the dancer a much more inspiring model than the professional and official ones whose commonplace, static poses they daily transferred to paper and canvas, or modeled in clay, in the drafty *ateliers* of the state school.

José Clara was one of that enraptured band of devotees of Isadora Duncan, and for more than two decades afterwards he continued to set down his linear impressions of the dancer's various creations. When in 1913 Fate's first foul blow struck the artist and it was thought that she might never again appear in public, Clara published some of his many drawings in a Paris art review. Accompanying the sketches he wrote a brief description of the impact which Isadora made upon her audiences in the 1902–3 performances.

"No stage set except long, neutral curtains which disappeared up into darkness and left the imagination free play. Of music: the best.

"When she appeared we all had the feeling that God—that is to say Certainty, Simplicity, Grandeur and Harmony—that God was present.

"She awakened or recreated all the fervors of the Ideal and of Art; the finest dreams and highest visions were born and unfolded through the magic of her movements.

Pastel sketches by Maurice Denis. Paris, ca. 1910. (*L'Art Décoratif*, August, 1913)

"Never was Prayer more ardent, Victory more irresistible, Virgin purer, Graces younger, Fury more tragic, Serenity more luminous than she—Isadora."

One is reminded here of the story told of Emerson and Margaret Fuller who had gone to see Fanny Ellsler during her tour of America in the 1840's. "Margaret," said the poet-philosopher, "this is poetry!" "Waldo," she corrected fervently, "this is religion."

Of these early appearances of Isadora before the Parisian public, another more detailed and literary account was written at the time by the dramatist, Henri Lavedan, then at the height of his fame. Like Elie Faure, the art historian, like Mario Meunier, the distinguished Hellenist, like the artists Carrière, Rodin, Bourdelle, Grandjouan, like the poet Fernand Divoire and a host of lesser figures, Lavedan could only speak of the new dancer in dithyrambic measures, piling up superlatives.

"On an empty stage, faintly lighted, unfurnished, simply and severely draped at the back and sides with a soft, blue fabric, a young woman, vital, beautiful, has been able without the aid of any artifice and without uttering a word, to hold an audience for two hours, in one of the largest theaters of Paris. She was alone, draped rather than dressed, and so simply that the tinted veils glorified rather than betrayed the vibrant yet statuesque beauty of her body. And the end of all this beauty and courage was to celebrate a Greek dance with bare feet; this she did with such spirit that she held a vast crowd alert, charmed, deeply moved and silent while the dance lasted. It was all accomplished before the most critical audience in the world by Isadora Duncan. . . .

"Imagine for yourself a woman with a body that suggests the perfection of Greek sculpture, without the slightest resemblance to the modern French figure. The proportions are so exquisite, so harmonious that one naturally relates the whole to the thought of a pedestal. . . . Straight, slender as a sapling, robust hips, with legs at once feminine and virile, bust fragile, with the shoulders of a young girl, arms charming and energetic and curving like a precious chaplet from finger to throat—the head of Athéna by Greuze. Thus to one's first astonished and enraptured gaze, Isadora appeared, without a suggestion of self-consciousness, yet slightly timid, modest but proud, her brow without a shadow and a faint smile in her eyes."

Such ecstatic praise naturally re-echoed throughout Europe and from her Parisian

Drawing in charcoal and white chalk by Maurice Denis as a study for the Champs-Elysées
theater murals. Paris, ca. 1910.

Isadora Duncan. Pen drawing by José Clara. Paris, ca. 1910.

Brush drawing by Abraham Walkowitz. New York, 1909.

triumphs Isadora danced across the continent to conquer in turn, Germany, Austria-
Hungary, Russia, Greece. Everywhere she went she was fêted; her press notices as she
once expressed it to me, were no mere prosaic criticisms but were poetic dithyrambs.
As always, the artists, delighting in her plastic beauty, sketched her, modeled her,
painted in oil and water-color, *"die göttliche, heilige Isadora."* Von Kaulbach, Schott,

49

Wash and ink drawings by Antoine Bourdelle. Paris, ca. 1916.

Bakst, Gordon Craig, are a few of the artists whose published representations of the dancer have come down to us from that first decade of the twentieth century.

Gordon Craig, then in Germany, was just beginning to evolve his theories of stage-craft and design; he was the first artist to publish in book form—or rather in large port-folio form—a series of studies of the young dancer. The very limited edition was published in Munich in 1906, the drawings having been done the year before. It was the forerunner of ten albums or books of drawings of Isadora done at various times and places, the latest being the Walkowitz pamphlet published only last year.

The second volume dedicated wholly to the dances of the American dancer was a strange collection of calligraphic sketches in pen and ink by a French artist, Jean-Paul

Théâtre des Champs-Elysées. Architecture by the brothers Perret. Sculptured reliefs by Antoine Bourdelle. Paris, 1913.

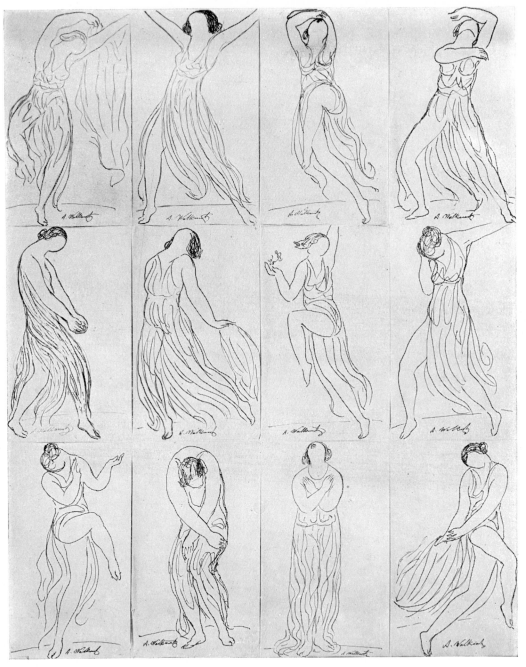

Pen and ink drawings of Isadora by Abraham Walkowitz. New York, 1920.

Lafitte. Published in the year 1910 by the then enterprising *Mercure de France*, it is notable for its preface from the pen of Elie Faure, the distinguished critic and art-historian. In part, Faure wrote:

"Yes, we wept when we saw her. It was no longer to our eyes, nor to our ears; it was no longer to our nerves that she spoke. From deep within us, when she danced, there arose a flood that swept away from the corners of our soul all the filth which had been piled up there by those who for twenty centuries had bequeathed to us their critique, their ethics, and their judgments. . . .

"When we eagerly watched her we rediscovered that primitive purity which, every two or three thousand years, reappears from the depth of the abyss of our worn-out conscience to restore a holy animality to us again. . . .

"Isadora! you have given us the certitude that the day is near when we shall once more come in fecund contact with instinctive life. You are the first flower of a tree still close to the earth and hidden among the old stripped trunks of a dying forest; but that tree will grow fiercely and scatter its seeds to make the forest thick and green again. . . . "

Faure had almost nothing to say of Lafitte's bold pen scratches. In most cases Lafitte had not cared about getting a likeness of the dancer; with a few quick strokes he sought to catch the swift movement of the limbs, the essential line of the gesture, the fall of the drapery about the body. His calligraphic scratches are a long way from the delicate yet precise line of many of the drawings made about the same time by André Dunoyer de Segonzac. To my mind that artist's line drawings are among the very finest drawings of the dance in general, or of Isadora Duncan in particular, done by any modern. They have been issued in book form in two albums, one dated 1910, the other 1913, and both are, like all the other early works about the dancer, collectors' items that are practically unobtainable.

The pastel drawings of the Frenchman, Grandjouan, also date from the same period as the Lafitte and de Segonzac ones and in their own way convey something more of the color and movement of the dancer's creations. Twenty-five of these studies were reproduced in facsimile on the same kind of colored hand-made paper originally used

Drawings in pen and ink by André Dunoyer de Segonzac. Paris, ca. 1911.

by the artist. They were bound in a very handsome hand-made album—about 48 inches by 30—of which only fifty copies were offered for sale to the public. As a contemporary advertisement in one of Isadora's programs announces: "Each album has an auto-graphed preface by Miss Duncan and is luxuriously bound in hand-tooled and hand-tinted leather. The copies are on sale at the price of 250 French francs ($50.00 at the rate of exchange then) at the author's Duncanschule at Marienhöhe, Darmstadt, and at M. Grandjouan's studio, 20 rue Poliveau, Paris."

It was during that brilliant Parisian period of the dancer's career—its apex, accord-ing to some critics—that the great sculptor, Emile-Antoine Bourdelle began to make his innumerable sketches. He first saw Isadora dance in public—apart from the Rodin fam-ily picnic in 1903—at a performance given in the Théâtre du Châtelet in 1909. From that moment on he was a devotee of the dancer and did an untold number of sketches of her, in the darkness of the theater, or at home in his *atelier*, recalling in tranquillity the divine movements which had given his sculptor's soul so much unalloyed pleasure.

In a letter dated September 10, 1912, written to Gabriel Thomas, Director of the Musée Grévin who had just been appointed to commission artists to decorate the new Théâtre des Champs-Elysées, then being constructed by the Perret brothers, Bourdelle recalls the occasion and says:

"To me it seemed that there, through her, was animated an ineffable frieze wherein divine frescoes slowly became human realities. Each leap, each attitude of the great artist remains in lightning flashes in my memory."

Later, at some soirée he saw Isadora again; she danced with the phenomenal star of the Ballets Russes—Nijinsky. In Bourdelle's private papers, notes of this evening were found.

"It seemed to me in my mind, as I watched Madame Isadora Duncan sitting or reclin-ing, that with each of her pauses she was offering me an antique marble throbbing with eternity. . . .

"I thought as I watched you: Phidias is working there.

"When you danced there was no break; it was like the seasons that follow one after the other in due course. . . .

Chalk drawing by Grandjouan. Paris, ca. 1924.  Pencil sketch by John Sloan. New York, ca. 1915. (The *Masses*, 1915)

"Miss Duncan was like an eternal priestess; evoking all the masterpieces of the noblest and highest antiquity, suscitating all the masterpieces to come and that through her superbly human heart."

Later, in 1913, Bourdelle again wrote:

"When the great Isadora Duncan danced before me, thirty years of my life looking at all the great human masterpieces became suddenly animated in these planes ordained from within by the spirit's aspiration."

As for Nijinsky, this is how the sculptor saw him:

"Nijinsky is filled with the dark effluvium of free animals. He is abrupt, but naïvely more than human, and he has something of the sacred animal."

56

When Bourdelle began to think about his bas-relief, "The Dance," for the façade of the Théâtre des Champs-Elysées, he noted down his first conception:

"The Dance is perhaps pretty, but it is also grave. It is like a meditation, at least I would like it to be so.

"Isadora, bending and throwing back her fine head, closes her eyes to dance within in her pure emotion.

"Her hands lightly touch the marble sky. They seem to die and their life pass away in well-arranged planes.

"He, the dancer, a Nijinsky, tears himself away with a wild leap from the marble still holding him fast. His bony feet are lifted far from the earth but the block will retain this man who carries within him the winged genius of the birds."

Speaking to some of his students long after the famous theater was built and decorated, Bourdelle said:

"All my muses in the theater are movements seized during Isadora's flight; she was my principal source.

"And all of you will have recognized Isadora Duncan who soars in my frieze beside the pensive Apollo whose lyre dictated her marvelous dance to her.

"With the nine different visages which I have been able to seize from many women's faces, it is still she, Isadora, who in my frieze clashes with Isadora, in the frenzy of the hymn or the surrender of the offering."

Thus it is that the Théâtre des Champs-Elysées—one of the most beautiful in the world—is in part a great monument to Isadora. For not only is she ever-present in all Bourdelle's work, in the bas-reliefs of the marble façade of the building; but within, her movements and the very folds of her tunic appear variously in many of the frescoes which decorate the entrance hall and the corridors. In the great circular auditorium itself she looks down in many different guises from the 16 meter panel "The Dance" above the stage and also from its 13 meter companion piece "The Symphony," two of the four great murals which Maurice Denis painted. Her influence is also there in the gilded bas-relief panel "The Dance," also by Maurice Denis, which shows six of her child dancers. She is there, too, on the decorative curtain, "Fête Dionysiaque," the

Pen drawing by José Clara. Paris,
ca. 1910.

Pen drawing from memory
by Robert Henri. New
York, ca. 1916.

work of K. X. Roussel, which hangs in the smaller Théâtre de la Comédie that adjoins the larger auditorium.

As has already been said, Bourdelle drew, both from life and from memory, innumerable sketches of Isadora. It was his intention at one time, I believe, to gather some of them into book form. Many of them had already been published in periodicals but a large group of the best, probably those selected for the proposed book, were left one day in a tramway by the absent-minded sculptor and were never recovered again. An essay by Elie Faure published in "La Revue de la Femme," in 1927 was probably intended, I should imagine from a certain indication in the text, as a preface to this volume. Faure's previous preface for the Lafitte studies published in 1910 has already been mentioned. His later piece, not only because of the author's increased eminence as an art historian and writer on esthetics, but because of his evaluation of the dancer and the sculptor's work, warrants being reprinted to the extent that space allows. I have therefore made the translation which follows:

"I have never experienced a livelier emotion than on the day when I saw Isadora dance for the first time. It increased the second time, perhaps, and was renewed the third. But after that it decreased each time. For I am forced to say, having written long ago a dithyrambic piece about her, that I no longer think of her today (1927) as I thought of her during the first days of the revelation.

"I came—quickly enough—to find that art didactic, wholly cultural, expressing only an interior life subtly set forth. It exhibited ideas, even principles, more than it expressed feeling or passions. It showed more knowledge than genius, more will than rapture, and less living harmonies than 'plastic equivalences.' Isadora demonstrated while dancing. In turn she indicated in an absolutely perfect way the Bacchante and the Suppliant, the Justiciary and the Warrior, the Virgin and the Seducer, and everything that might be most definite and fully defined. I confess that the slightest Spanish dancer, thin, nervous, black as a dried olive, has more spiritual flame in her convulsive little finger than ever had that great body, sculptural as ever female body could be. The American dancer had studied dancing on the flanks of vases. But the Ronda dancer carried the dance in her own flanks. One had the unlimited sense of voluptuousness, death and universal vanity; the other had the exact sense of the art.

"I had come to think this of the great artist. But before the atrocious fate which tried to make her an ill-starred woman, I revised my judgment. . . . Pity made me more just. She conquered, by the silent command of my heart, the protest of my mind—which I had thought steadfast—against the glory that shone about the astonishing creature. I had wished to see a virtuoso in the dancer. I discovered an animator in the woman.

"It is she whom I discover in the stubborn mask drawn by Bourdelle. She created an immense movement. In the wake of the illusions she scattered like a sower, she caused to sprout in the souls of poets, dancers, sculptors, painters, and in the anonymous masses, so many emotions that are not visible but echo from place to place, creating a state of collective sensibility where the seed grows effortlessly. She rehabilitated the dance, forgotten or unknown, the humble and glorious dance, guardian, with song and popular pottery, of the concrete genius of races, ceaselessly deformed and slandered by professional artists. It was she who, in the West, preceded the triumphal entry of the Russian dancers. It was she who opened the way to the secret passages which unite by so many interwoven undulations, music and plastic art. It was she who prepared the way for the enthronement of rhythm alone, as a permanent factor of esthetic mystery, on the ruins of naturalism, academicism, romanticism, classicism, and in general of all the schools which, above everything else, attempt to represent the object. Without doubt she helped the nascent cinema to discover its real sense outside the theater, outside the imitation of forms, in that single silent empire of rhythm where dancing, painting, sculpture, and music confusedly meet.

"This great esthetic drama which washes over us and toward which, more than anyone else, Isadora has impelled us, none has lived it better than Bourdelle with his double genius wherein the most spontaneous symbolism that ever was in sculpture is locked in an ardent embrace with the sensual and realistic craft of the most accomplished of craftsmen. Two faculties which often in him express the most heartrending of the tragedies of the intelligence, that flow one over the other or join in an endless struggle where one downs the other; at other times impetuously mounting together to twist, in a single sheaf, the fuel and the fire."

Thus far I have only spoken of the European artists who drew, painted, and modeled Isadora Duncan. And that because chronologically they come before the American artists; also, in quality and quantity their work is often far superior to that done by the dancer's compatriots. Isadora, however, was not ignored by the artists of America, nor did her dance go unappreciated or unlimned.

One of her earliest admirers was the eminent Chicago sculptor, Lorado Taft. To him she was, he said: "Poetry personified. She is not the Tenth Muse but all the Nine Muses in one—and painting and sculpture as well."

Robert Henri was also among the first and most articulate of her admirers among the band of artists who acclaimed her upon her first American tour after her European triumphs. He spoke of her as "perhaps one of the greatest masters of gesture the world has

Crayon drawing by Van Deering Perrine, ca. 1920. (Used as a program cover for Isadora's Russian tour of 1921.)

ever seen." She "carries us through a universe in a single movement of her body. Her hand alone held aloft becomes a shape of infinite significance." "Isadora Duncan," he said again, "dances and fills the universe. She exceeds all ordinary measure."

Another artist of the period who did many and, according to those who remember them, superb drawings of the dancer, was the painter Arthur B. Davies. Unfortunately they were all destroyed in a fire which occurred in the artist's studio. Luckier than Davies has been the painter, Abraham Walkowitz. He also, dating from that period, made an uncountable number of sketches of his favorite dancer. But he has seen to it that they have been placed in the safekeeping of such sure custodians as the print departments of museums and libraries.

Last year Walkowitz crowded together a vast collection of these sketches into an over-size pamphlet, which despite the laudable intentions of the artist, cannot be said to stand up alongside the European publications. Whatever the merits of the drawings—and some of Walkowitz's first drawings were done with obvious emotional fire and technical surety—the lack of typographical taste with which they are set forth in this pamphlet takes away much of their value.

Drawings by two American artists were especial favorites of Isadora. One chalk drawing by Van Deering Perrine she used on the cover of her programs at the Century Theatre in New York during the Spring season in 1915, at the Metropolitan Opera House in 1916, and several times in Russia. A pen and ink drawing of "Les Funerailles" by Ruth Reeves—one of a series done during the 1920 season at the Théâtre des Champs-Elysées—was used as a program cover during a *tournée* in Belgium and Holland a few years later.

Mention should surely be made here of the photographic studies of Isadora Duncan made by two Americans and unsurpassed by any others made abroad. Arnold Genthe's many studies of the dancer and her creations—some of these were published in book form in 1928—and the Acropolis series done by Edward Steichen, are not at all dwarfed in the presence of works in other pictorial mediums done by some of the world's greatest artists. Both Genthe and Steichen have raised photography, to quote the former, "from the mechanical lifeless medium it had become, to the dignity and status of a real art."

In looking over the diverse studies of the dancer done at various periods by these two Americans, one can only regret that neither photographer ever had the necessary equipment or the foresight to film at least one of the dance creations of Isadora—the ineffable little waltz, say, to the music of Brahms (Op. 39), or the mighty and tragic *Marche Slave* of Chaikovsky. As the poet Shaemas O'Sheel has said: "A few reels of film, by which the presence, the rhythm, the grace, the imperious gesture of Isadora could be evoked at will, immediate and mobile—what a treasure they would be!"

Since that treasure has been denied us we must be content with what has been bequeathed to us by Rodin and Bourdelle and de Segonzac and Clara and the happy host of great men who saw her, and had the ready wit and pictorial talent to set down for future generations some of the beauty and the magic of the Daughter of Dionysus, Isadora Duncan.

STUDIO ISADORA DUNCAN
343, PROMENADE DES ANGLAIS — NICE

— MARDI 14 SEPTEMBRE 1926 à 5 heures —

RÉCITAL JEAN COCTEAU
AVEC LE CONCOURS D'ISADORA DUNCAN
DE L'AUTEUR ET DE MARCEL HERRAND

Program cover for public re-
cital. Pen drawing by Jean Cocteau. Nice, 1926.

# Isadora Duncan: Studies for Six Dance Movements

## BY GORDON CRAIG

### PROLOGUE

Much noise and deep restlessness
Grief and disharmony
Is this the whole end of it?
The truth of it all?
Is it so certain then that this life
Consists only of fourfold nonsense?
Is it not far more true that this life
Is exactly the reverse,
Rest—joy and harmony,
Rhythm, the most certain truth—
And the expression of all this—Art?
Is evil then, and ugliness,
Really the image of force?
Must restlessness be the symbol of life—
Must a noisy, trying gloom spread
Over the enchantment of things—
If these are questions, I do not ask questions—
For I have no doubts at all,—

I see calmness and beauty, the strong and sweet
Draw near in a perfect manner—
Everything gives place to the spirit,
Nothing can hinder it—
Three lines or three hundred
Give the same picture—
One tone or a staff of tones
The same melody
One step or a hundred steps
Create the same dance.
Something set down—
As a record—
Something uttered on the divine theme,
Which is so simple and only simple to comprehend—
The theme which commences
"I am happy. . . . "
And ends with
". . . how fair."
This is what she dances—
Never yet has she shown dark or unbearable sorrow—
Always sunshine's around her—
Even the little shadows disappear
And flee, when she passes—
This is the real force—
She springs from the Great Race—
From the Great Companions—
From the line of Sovereigns, who
Maintain the world and make it move,
From the Courageous Giants,
The Guardians of Beauty—
The Solvers of all Riddles.

Leipzig, 1906
*Translated by George Amberg*

STRAUSS

PERI

CHOPIN

GLUCK

BEETHOVEN

Pastel drawing of Isadora by Gordon Craig, ca. 1904. (Courtesy George Chaffee collection)

# CHRONOLOGY

1878   Born San Francisco, May 27.

1890   Danced in Augustin Duncan's San Francisco Barn Theater.

1892–4   Gave dancing lessons in San Francisco.

1896   Left for Chicago. Danced for theater managers and then in a roof garden under an assumed name.

1896   Met Augustin Daly in Chicago. He engaged her to dance in *Midsummer Night's Dream*, New York.

1896   Concerts in the Carnegie Hall Studio with Ethelbert Nevin.

1899   To London on cattle boat under the assumed name of O'Gorman.
British Museum visits. Read Winckelman's *Journey to Athens;* sketched Greek vases. Danced in private homes.
Met Andrew Lang, translator of Homer, and G. G. Watts.

1900   First visit to Paris. Visited Rodin Pavilion at the International Exposition of 1900.
Daily visits to the Louvre. Victory of Samothrace; Venus de Milo.
Danced in the studio of the Princess de Polignac.
Visited Rodin's studio.

1902   First visits to Leipzig and Munich. Saw Loie Fuller dance.

1903   *First contract to dance* in a public theater. Thirty nights, Urania Theater, Budapest. Great success.

1904   Debut at Kroll Opera House, Berlin.
First visits to Italy and Greece; plans to settle in Athens.

1905   In Vienna to present the choruses of *The Suppliants* of Aeschylus with Greek boy's chorus.
Left Berlin for St. Petersburg.
Saw the ballerina Mathilde Kschesinskya and admired her. Met Diaghilev, Bakst, Benois, Stanislavsky. Visited the Imperial Ballet School. Visited Moscow.
Returned to Berlin. Opened a school in Grunewald with her sister Elizabeth.
Met Gordon Craig, the great stage designer, in Berlin.

1906   To the Scandinavian countries. Not impressed by the Gymnastic Studio at Stockholm.
Her first child by Craig born in Holland.
To Florence: saw Duse in Craig's production of Ibsen's *Rosmersholm*.

1907    Toured Russia.

1908    London.

To New York. Danced Gluck's *Iphigenia,* August, 1908.

Met George Grey Barnard, Belasco, the painters Robert Henri and George Bellows, the poet Max Eastman.

Danced with Walter Damrosch and Symphony Orchestra before continental tour, December, 1908, Metropolitan Opera House.

1909    Returned to Paris.

Under direction of Lugné-Poe gave a series of successful concerts in Paris.

Met Paris Singer.

1911    Returned to America. Danced with Damrosch Symphony.

1912    Met d'Annunzio in Paris, 1912.

1913    Her children drowned in France.

1914    Began her school at Bellevue, outside Paris; presented her pupils at the Trocadéro in June, 1914.

1915    Returned to New York. Rented studio at Fourth Avenue and 23rd Street.

Improvised *La Marseillaise* at the Metropolitan Opera House.

Left the United States for Naples.

1916    Sailed for South American tour.

Returned to New York to give performances at the Metropolitan.

1917    Returned to California after twenty-two years.

1918    Returned to Paris.

1920    Revisited Athens with the hope of creating a school again.

1921    Received an invitation from the Soviet government to establish a school of dancing in Moscow.

1922    Married the Russian poet, Serge Essenin, May 3.

Visited Elizabeth Duncan's school at Potsdam.

Danced at the Théâtre de la Monnaie in Brussels.

Arrived in France, the first Soviet citizen to enter.

Came to New York with her husband and was detained at Ellis Island.

Gave three sell-out concerts at Carnegie Hall; performances in Boston and Indianapolis.

1923    Returned to France in February.

1924    Arrived in Moscow with Essenin.

1927    Returned to Paris and gave last concert at the Théâtre Mogador, July 8.

Killed at Nice, September 14.

# BIBLIOGRAPHY OF ISADORA DUNCAN

## A LIST OF REFERENCES IN AMERICAN LIBRARIES

ADAMS, MILDRED. Isadora Duncan: rhythmic way to beauty. *In* Women citizen mag. 11:26–27. New York, Oct., 1926.

The ART of Isadora Duncan. *In* Review of reviews. 63:407. London, May, 1921.

The ART of the dance. Isadora Duncan. Edited with an introduction by Sheldon Cheney. New York, Theatre Arts, Inc. 1928. 147 pages. illus. (Essays on the dance of Isadora by Max Eastman, Eva LeGallienne, Robert Edmond Jones, and others.)

ATTEMPT to awaken an art that has slept for two thousand years. *In* Current literature. Vol. 45:556–558. New York, Nov., 1908. (On the dance of Isadora Duncan.)

BEINSTOCK, J. W. Isadora's Russian husband. *In* Living age. 333:925–928. Boston, Nov., 1927.

BENGOECHA, HERNAN DE. Isadora Duncan. *In* Revista de America. 2:113–121. Paris, 1913.

BOLITHO, WILLIAM. Isadora Duncan. *In his* Twelve against the gods. . . . New York, Simon & Schuster, 1929. pp. 302–327.

BYRONIANAS, AGNES. Como conoci i Isadora Duncan. *In* Revista de revistas. pp. 20–24. April 20, 1930.

CAFFIN, CHARLES H. Henri Matisse and Isadora Duncan. *In* Camera work. 25:17–20. New York, 1929.

CLARA Y AYRATS, JOSE. Isadora Duncan; soixante-douze planches par José Clara, avec une présentation de George A. Denis. Paris, Editions Reider, 1928. 9 pages, plates.

——. Isadora Duncan. *In* L'Art décoratif. 15:103–108. illus. Paris, 1913.

CLASSIC dances of Isadora Duncan. *In* Green book album. 1:137–140. Chicago, Jan., 1909.

CORTISSOZ, ROYAL. Isadora Duncan. Reflections apropos of her work. *In* New music review. 8:201–204. New York, Mar., 1909.

CRAIG, EDWARD GORDON. Isadora Duncan. Sechs bewegungstudien, 1906. Leipzig, Inselverlag, 1906.

DELL, FLOYD. Olive Schreiner and Isadora Duncan. *In his* Women as world builders. Chicago, Forbes, 1913. pp. 41–51.

DER LING, PRINCESS. A pupil of Isadora. *In* Mentor. 22:18–20, 61. illus. New York, Sept., 1930.

DESTI, MARY. Isadora Duncan's end. London, V. Gollancz, 1929. 351 pages. illus.

——. The untold story, the life of Isadora Duncan, 1921–1927. New York, Liveright, 1929. 281 pages. illus.

DIVOIRE, FERNAND. La revolution d'Isadora Duncan. *In* Les spectacles A travers les ages. Paris, 1932. pp. 215–234. illus.

——. Isadora Duncan: Obituaire. *In* L'Illustration. 85:317. Paris, Sept. 24, 1927.

——. Isadora Duncan, fille de Promethée . . . decorées par E. A. Bourdelle. Paris Editions des muses Françaises, 1919. 58 pages. illus.

DOWD, HAROLD. The art of Isadora Duncan. *In* Theatre guild mag. 6:51–52. New York, Feb., 1929.

DUMESNIL, MAURICE. An amazing journey. Isadora Duncan in South America. New York, Ives Washburn, 1932. 311 pages. illus.

DUNCAN, IRMA. The technique of Isadora Duncan. New York, Kamin publishers, 1937. 35 pp. illus. facsim.

DUNCAN, IRMA, and MACDOUGALL, A. R. Isadora Duncan's Russian days and her last years in France, by Irma Duncan and Alice R. Macdougall. New York, Covici-Friede, 1929. 371 pp. illus.

DUNCAN, ISADORA. My life. New York, Liveright, 1927. 359 pp. illus.

——. Ma vie par Isadora Duncan. Traduit de l'anglais par Jean Allery. Paris, Librarie Gallimard, 1928. 382 pages. (My life: French text.)

——. Isadora Duncan. Memoriem. Mit 137 Abbildungen. Nach den englischen manuskript bearbeitet von C. Zell. Zurich, etc., Amalthea-verlag, 1928. 410 pp. illus. (My life: German text.)

——. . . . Mana dzive, tulkojis R. Deisons. Riga: "Gramatu draugs" 1934. 280 pp. plats. (My life: Lettish text.)

——. Moya shizn'. Perevod Ya. Yakovleva. Moskva:izdat., "Federatziya," 1930. xi–298 pp. (My life: Russian text.)

——. Mémoires d'Isadora Duncan Amour, musique et danse. *In* La revue musicale. 9:97–116. Paris, Mar., 1928. illus.

——. The dance. Introduction by Mary Fanton Roberts. *In* Touchstone mag. 2:3–16. New York, Oct., 1917.

——. The dance in relation to tragedy. *In* Theatre arts monthly. 11:755–761. New York, Oct., 1927.

——. Dancing in relation to religion and love. *In* Theatre arts monthly. 9:584–593. New York, Aug., 1927.

——. Der Tanz der zukunft (The dance of the future), eine vorlesung; übersetz und eingeleitet von Karl Federn. Leipzig, E. Diedrichs, 1930. 46 pp.

——. The dance. Authorized edition. New York, The Forest press, 1909. 28 pp. illus.

The DUNCAN dancers from Moscow. *In* Literary digest. 100:23. New York, Jan. 19, 1929.

EASTMAN, MAX. Isadora Duncan is dead. *In* Nation. 125:309. New York, Sept., 1927.

ECRITS sur la danse. Manuscripts inédits et textes communiqués par, Ch. Dallies, Fernand Divoire, Mario Menuier, Georges Delaquys, et illustrées de dessins in édits par A. Bourdelle, José Clara et Grandjouan. Paris, Grenier, 1927. 85 pp. illus.

ETSCHER, GASPARD. The renaissance of the dance. Isadora Duncan. *In* Forum mag. 46:322–329. Sept., 1911.

EVAN, BLANCHE. Isadora Duncan. Road to the dance. *In* Theatre arts monthly. 19:27–34. New York, Jan., 1935.

FORD, J. E. Isadora Duncan. *In* Putnam's mag. 5:481. New York, Jan., 1909. (A poem.)

FREEMAN, HELEN. Isadora. *In* Theatre arts monthly. 11:942. New York, Dec., 1927. (A poem.)

FREJAVILLE, G. Isadora Duncan. *In* Jour. des débats politiques et litteraires. 34:531–532. Paris, Sept. 23, 1927.

GOLD, MICHAEL. The loves of Isadora. *In* New masses. 4:20–21. New York, Mar., 1929.

HOWARD, RUTH ELEANOR. Isadora Duncan "In Memoriam." *In* American dancer. Los Angeles, Oct., 1927. pp. 11, 30. port.

ISADORA Duncan's Art. *In* Literary digest. 50:1018–1019. New York, May, 1915.

——. *In* Outlook. 147:103–104. New York, Sept. 28, 1927.

ISADORA Duncan's artistic credo. *In* Literary digest. 95:28–29. New York, Oct. 8, 1927.

ISADORA Duncan dancers. *In* Le Théâtre et Comoedia Illustré. Paris, Feb., 1922, no. 2, p. 141. (A note on the concert of Anna, Lisa and Erica Duncan, with illustrations.)

——. *In* Le Théâtre et Comoedia Illustré. 2:141. Paris, Feb., 1922.

ISADORA Duncan dances the Marseillaise. *In* Current opinion. 62:31. New York, Jan., 1917.

ISADORA Duncan's triumphs and tragedies. *In* Literary digest. 95:48–52. New York, Oct., 1927.

ISADORA Duncan's Moscow school. *In* Le Théâtre et Comoedia Illustré. 39:649–652. Paris, Nov., 1924.

ISADORA Duncan. *In* Comoedia Illustré. pp. 122–123. Paris, Feb., 1909. (A note on her concert.)

——. *In* Comoedia Illustré. 3:269. Paris, Feb., 1911. (A note on her concert at the Châtelet.)

——. *In* The Theatre . . . 8:324. New York, Dec., 1908. (A poem to Isadora by Charles H. Towne.)

——. *In* The Theatre. 3:184. New York, Aug., 1903. port.

——. *In* The Theatre. 14:122. New York, Oct., 1911. (A poem to Isadora.)

——. *In* Comoedia Illustré. 4:321. Paris, Feb., 1912.

——. Obituary. *In* Theatre arts monthly. 11:842–843. New York, Nov., 1927.

ISADORA Duncan and Pavlova. *In* Harper's weekly. 58:5. New York, Nov. 29, 1913.

ISADORA Duncan: dessins de Albertine Bernouard, René Piot et Louis Sue; hors-texte de Antoine Bourdelle, José Clara et Grandjouan. Paris, G. Labruyere, 19—.

——. An episode in her career. *In* Harper's mag. 158:246–249. New York, Jan., 1929.

KAYE, JOSEPH. The last chapters of Isadora's life. *In* Dance mag. 12:21–24; 30–33; 36–39. New York, April–July, 1929.

KINEL, LOLA. This is my affair . . . Boston, Little, Brown, 1937. xxv–335 pp. illus. (Autobiography of Isadora Duncan's secretary.)

LAFITTE, JEAN-PAUL. Les danses d'Isadore Duncan; avec une préface de Elie Faure. Paris, Mercure de France, 1910. 14 pp. 36 plates.

LALOY, LOUIS. Isadora Duncan et la danse nouvelle. *In* La revue musicale. 4:249–253. Paris, May, 1904.

LEVEIN, SONYA. The art of Isadora Duncan. *In* Metropolitan mag. 42:38–39. New York, June, 1915.

LEVINSON, ANDRE. Isadora Duncan. *In his* La danse d'aujourd'hui . . . Paris, Editions Duchartre et Van Buggenhoudt, 1929. pp. 142–161.

LUGNE-POE. Isadora Duncan . . . et nos Oeuvriers. *In* Revue politique et litteraire. 71:3–8. Paris, Jan., 1933.

LUHAN, MABEL DODGE. Isadora Duncan—Elizabeth Duncan—The Elizabeth Duncan school. *In her* Movers and shakers. New York, Harcourt, Brace, 1936. pp. 319–348.

——. Isadora Duncan. *In* New English weekly. pp. 396–399. London, Aug. 11, 1932.

MACDONALD, CLAIRE. Isadora Duncan. *In* Home and abroad. 8:124–126. London, Spring, 1929.

MACDOUGALL, A. R. Dancer speaks. *In* Touchstone mag. 8:336–339. New York, Feb., 1921. (A note on Isadora.)

MARSH, LUCILE. The shadow of Wigman in the light of Duncan. *In* Dance mag. pp. 12–13, 62. New York, May, 1931.

MASON, ARTHUR. Mistress of the dance. *In* Green book album. 1:137–140. Chicago, Jan., 1909.

MEEUS, MARIE-LOUISE DE. A star danced: Isadora Duncan and Anna Pavlova. *In* Cornhill mag. 72:544–551. London, May, 1932.

MESTRE, JULIA. Isadora Duncan. *In* Revista de la facultad de letras y ciencias. 30:385–395. Havana, 1921.

MILLE, PIERRE. Isadora Duncan. *In* Le Théâtre. 244:20–21. Paris, Feb., 1909. illus.

MISS Isadora Duncan en haar school te Gruenwald bij Berlin. *In* Elsevier's Geillus. maandschrift. 32:88–102. Amsterdam, 1906.

MISS Isadora Duncan's matinees at the Prince of Wales Theatre, London. *In* Spectator. 126: 524–525. London, April 23, 1921.

NEWMAN, ERNEST. Dances of Isadora Duncan. *In* Living age. 309:606–607. Boston, June, 1921.

MONROE, HARRIET. Isadora Duncan: Golden moments. *In* Poetry mag. 31:206–207. New York, Jan., 1928.

NORMAN, GERTRUDE. Appreciation of Isadora Duncan. *In* The Theatre. 5:36–39. New York, Feb., 1905.

O'SHEEL, SHAEMUS. Isadora Duncan, priestess. *In* Poet lore. 21:480–492. Boston, Nov., 1910.

PARKER, H. T. Isolated Isadora. *In his* Eight notes; voices and figures of music and the dance. New York, Dodd, Mead, 1922. pp. 231–238.

PAVLOVA, NELIA. Essenine et Isadora Duncan. *In* Revue mondiale. pp. 63–66. Paris, Jan., 1930.

PICKERING, RUTH. Isadora Duncan. *In* Nation. 128:202–204. New York, Feb., 1929.

ROBERTS, MARY FANTON. The dance of the future as created and illustrated by Isadora Duncan. *In* Craftsman mag. 13:48–56. New York, Oct., 1908. illus.

——. France honors Isadora Duncan and helps her to establish a free school of dancing. *In* Touchstone mag. 7:303–309. New York, July, 1920.

RUHL, ARTHUR. Some ladies who dance. *In* Collier's mag. 44:17–18. New York, Feb., 1910.

A RUSSIAN's opinion of Isadora Duncan. *In* Living age. 323:401–402. Boston, Nov. 15, 1924.

SAURET, HENRIETTE. Isadora Duncan, impératrice errante. *In* Revue mondiale. pp. 161–172. Paris, Mar., 1928.

SCHREIBER, GERHARDT. Arthur Nikisch und Isadora Duncan. *In* Der Tanz. pp. 22–23. Berlin, May, 1929.

SECHAN, LOUIS. Isadora Duncan. *In his* La danse grecque antique . . . Paris, E. de Boccan, 1930. pp. 315–357.

SELDES, GEORGE. What love meant to Isadora. *In* Mentor mag. 18:25–27; 64–65. Springfield, Ohio, Feb., 1930.

SERGINES. Les Echos: Isadora Duncan. *In* Annales politiques et litteraires. 89:322. Paris, Oct. 1, 1927.

STOKES, SEWELL. Isadora Duncan; an intimate portrait. London, Brentano, 1928. 208 pp. illus.

SVETLOV, VALERIEN. Duncan. *In his* Le ballet contemporain . . . St. Petersburg, 1912. pp. 61–84.

To Isadora Duncan: a tribute from a young student. *In* Touchstone mag. 7:307–308. New York, July, 1920.

VAN VECHTEN, CARL. The new Isadora. *In his* Merry-go-round . . . New York, A. Knopf, 1918. pp. 307–317.

WERNER, MORRIS R. Isadora Duncan. *In his* To whom it may concern. New York, Cape & Smith, 1931. pp. 245–277.

YORSKA, MME. Isadora Duncan. What she hopes to achieve in the future. *In* Arts and decoration. 27:46, 80. New York, Aug., 1927.

YOUNG, STARK. Isadora Duncan. *In* New republic. 57:43–44. New York, Nov. 28, 1928.

Bookplate monogram (I. D.).
Woodcut by Gordon Craig, ca. 1906.

# ALBUMS AND BOOKS OF DRAWINGS OF ISADORA DUNCAN

ALGI, VAN SAANEN. Isadora Duncan. A book of line drawings. Paris. 1920(?).

BOURDELLE, EMILE-ANTOINE. Isadora Duncan, Fille de Promethée. Water-color and line drawings with poems by Fernand Divoire. Les Muses Françaises. Paris. 1919.

CLARA, JOSÉ. Isadora Duncan.* An album of 72 plates. Drawings in water-color and line. Preface in French by Georges Denis. Reider. Paris. 1928.

CRAIG, EDWARD GORDON. Sechs Bebegungstudien.* An album of six lithographic drawings, each matter and loose. Prologue in German. Limited Edition. Leipzig. 1906.

DE SEGONZAC, ANDRE DUNOYER. Dessins sur les danses d'Isadora Duncan précédés de La Danseuse de Diane. Line drawings. (Preface in French by Fernand Divoire.) Limited Edition. La Belle Edition. Paris. 1910.

——. XXX Dessins:* Line drawings of Isadora alone and with her child dancers. (Also a few of Ida Rubinstein, and some studies of boxers.) Limited Edition. Les Editions du Temps Present. Paris. 1913.

GRANDJOUAN. A series of 25 colored pastel facsimiles on colored, hand-made paper. Paris. 1913(?).

JACQUES, LUCIEN. Isadora Duncan. A book of line drawings. Paris. 1920(?).

LAFITTE, JEAN-PAUL. Les Danses d'Isadora Duncan. A book of line drawings. 38 Plates. In four sections: The Religious Dances; The Vases; The Bacchantes; The Return of the Warriors. Preface in French by Elie Faure. Mercure de France. 1910.

WALKOWITZ, ABRAHAM. Isadora Duncan in her Dance.* Pamphlet of water-color and line drawings. Forewords by Mary Fanton Roberts, Maria-Theresa, Carl Van Vechten, Arnold Genthe and Shaemus O'Sheel. Haldeman-Julius. Kansas City, 1945.

# PHOTOGRAPHS

GENTHE, ARNOLD. 24 Photographic studies of Isadora Duncan.* Foreword by Max Eastman. Mitchel Kennerly. New York and London. 1929.

* In the Department of Dance and Theatre Design, Museum of Modern Art, New York City.

Isadora as a member of the Augustin Daly Theatrical Company. New York, 1896.

Portrait study of Isadora Duncan.
Paris, ca. 1900.

Chicago, ca. 1896.

Portrait study. Munich, 1903.

New York, 1922.

82

Portrait study by Arnold Genthe. New York, 1916.

Isadora's studio in Moscow. Moscow, 1924.

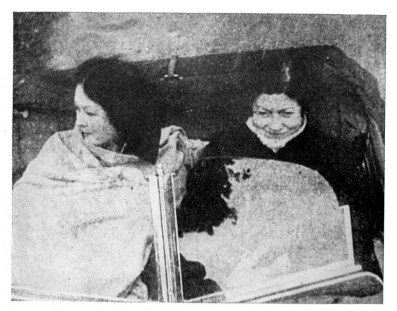

Isadora Duncan and her companion (Mary Desti) in the car in which she was killed. Taken the day before her death. From a snap-shot owned by Martha Graham. Photographer unknown. Nice, September 13, 1927. (Courtesy Martha Graham and Barbara Morgan)